S155

NO GRAVE CAN HO

O MY BODY DOWN

AHSAHTA PRESS
BOISE, IDAHO

2011

THE NEW SERIES

#42

NO GRAVE CAN HOLD MY BODY DOWN

AARON McCOLLOUGH

Ahsahta Press, Boise State University, Boise, Idaho 83725-1525

http://ahsahtapress.boisestate.edu

http://ahsahtapress.boisestate.edu/books/mccollough3/mccollough3.htm

Cover design by Quemadura

Cover photograph © Black River Productions, Ltd. / Mitch Epstein.

Courtesy of Sikkema Jenkins & Co., New York. Used with permission. All rights reserved.

Book design by Janet Holmes

Printed in Canada

LIBRARY OF CONGRESS CATALOGING-IN-PUBLICATION DATA

McCollough, Aaron.
No grave can hold my body down / Aaron McCollough.
p. cm. — (The new series #42)
ISBN-13: 978-1-934103-22-7 (pbk. : alk. paper)
ISBN-10: 0-916272-90-7 (pbk. : alk. paper)
I. Title.
PS3613.C37N6 2011
811′.6—DC22
2011016468

ACKNOWLEDGMENTS

Sections of this manuscript have appeared in *Practice, CutBank, The Green Integer Review, Interim, Fascicle, Word For/Word, Free Verse, Wherever We Put Our Hats,* and *MiPoesias.*

NOTE

"Amazing Grace": The definition of "Wretch" is taken from The Online Etymology Dictionary,
http://www.etymonline.com/

Contents

What can oppose the decline of the west
is not a resurrected culture
but the utopia that is silently contained
in the image of its decline.

—Theodor Adorno, *Prisms*

Jesus is a dying bed maker
Jesus is a dying
is Jesus   aiding
the dying among the dying
a Jesus is
making die   easing us
into dying   Jesus is a bed
ache   a bad bed
buried with him by
baptism into death
us is a dying   a bit of me
in bed with dying   by us
married to another
us who walk after
the flesh
Jesus is a dying bed maker
as we rise from bed
what are we   walking for
add Jesus   bed Jesus   die
be made as a bed is made
first the fitted sheet then
the flat and finally a blanket
fresh rather rough cotton
or light flannel
and tear the sheets away
in an ague
the use of pleasure is
a dying bed maker
the use of ache and dying is
the ease of dying   the ache of
rising makes
the flesh   the flesh makes
a dying bed maker

"Jesus Is a Dying Bedmaker"

I see right through my death to the limit
in the lotus blossom of the dust box

down the stack (arpeggios of good/bad)
what does it unravel in dry cornhusks
to long calligraphic comfort against
tribulation tribulation make me
make me bed me man of sorrows lover

in cold clothes Jesus
in the country under INRI

as I cannot move
I rise with love and just peer past the sash
to all so splendid the shroud you've made me

so concerned with my own spirit
the details of the day went sharp brilliant
and went sharp dark

so concerned I was scrupulously full
of care in the morning tight in my sheets
my pallor was my day the death in day

*

I am blue lord with pallor blue today
waiting for the countenance up or down
and the tuning of strings how can I pray
with these fingers or anything of mine

sick with seeing right through to the return
to my america in which I am
my nation's pale blue shadow turning in
the sheets the fire in my shoulder the yard

the giant lawn of the nation body
prison way of being in creation

american prison of the soul, lord,
I love or not, how do I love from here

when I have seen you is it as others
see you cougar and crocodile entwined

*

but my heart is a mess in my fingers
my country is no child I am no child
in the rain in the snow the rain the snow

clinging to everything the dew the yard
from curb to curb the car lengths to heaven

*

Charley Patton, well

Stretch me from corner to corner
Lord, break my heart for
Stretch me from toe to finger
Kiss me on my mouth
I've got religion
But

Well

*

rivers
at my feet, lord, a delta and a spring
crenulated like a leaf of waters
the plash of the wheel working my fever
to your cool hands Jesus your cool morphine
I may just shut my eyes for a moment

The sky is gray. The weather is threatening. The light is changing. It must be about 6 p.m. Through the giant lawn of rural Pennsylvania a thin road bends and rises and dips. In the distance there are hills. In the middle ground a small valley but from where I stand the landscape looks awkwardly compressed as it edges up against me.

The light of the stars taking so long to get here: this is how the dead see the living world when they rise.

Through the giant lawn of middle Tennessee a thin road bends and rises and dips. The hills and valleys are so compressed that the bend looks more like an angle: an impossibly sharp one. I know there are differences between these two places: different words are being spoken in the houses behind the scrubby pines and it's hotter on this road. Different patterns appear in the cracks of that road. I know these differences exist, but I cannot sense them. A road bends and rises and dips in Tennessee. A road bends and rises and dips in Pennsylvania. A road bends and rises and dips.

I am on a road.

Before Edwin Budding 1830, grass had to be managed with a scythe or with grazing beasts. The typical American yard was a mixture of different weeds when Whitman was composing *Leaves of Grass*. It was a scraggly garden of plantain, henbit, creeping pale, barberry, and multiflora rose. A kind of meadow in miniature. Where it grew, grass tended to grow unchecked. It got exceptionally tall. *The beautiful uncut hair of graves.*

"Amazing Grace"

In this garden I cannot see

*

Wretch, from O.E. *wrecca* "wretch, stranger, exile," related to *wrec-can* "to drive out, punish" (see *wreak*). Sense of "vile, despicable person" developed in O.E., reflecting the sorry state of the outcast, as presented in much of Anglo-Saxon verse (*e.g.* "The Wanderer"). A Ger. word for "misery" is *Elend,* from O.H.G. *elilenti* "sojourn in a foreign land, exile."

All lovers lord are wretched look them up
they swim the fountains of gardens to touch
to grasp the fountain to kiss the white dusk
I am such a one was such a one am
I   safe in the lawn is the campus safe
from ghosts dearth of fear of ghosts proper fear
the yo-yo of desire should still instill
like an hammered *A*: one never belongs
not even in one's room   "one's room" owning
not folding the note nor saving the note
not even in giving the note away

right here in my easy homeland I
am afraid and feel their eyes upon me
america   an amazing tiger
did you make it did you make me and it
the good cloth armor of the wretched self
that I was such a senseless man of wants
in a land in love with want in want of fear
afraid to be afraid

All lovers long for death   the heresy
of devotion is so great   am I safe
from fear of this   from fear of ghosts of acts
but am I safe lord from love's destruction

the book of acts

golden beets they're bringing the philosopher's club
and backwards on his horse now the one who prates

Eimi ho eimi, who falls and says "it happened"
added later: "what happens to us" in athens

all shattered, in ad hoc stacks, thinking like pseudo-nicodemus
I am the seed in the blood *semen in sanguis*

top o' the worl' like so many athletes of piety
I am the remnant what history was on about

torn in pieces of wilde beastes, beheaded, stoned,
stifled, beaten to death with cudgels, ravished with zeal

they bring us beets bunched
from these busted porches the olive oil leaking

added later: "what happens to us"
"beloved, a night and a day in the deep"

until the iamb *dazzle of the poplars*
emptied out unto the acts *uninherit*

in here they bring us radishes like hands
on iron chargers or generation of vipers

Eulalia's soul flies from her mouth as a dove
over offal awful, awesome sandscapes

whereof let every reader use her judgment
hear her rattle like the grocery bag down the walk

and the popping sound of convictions ablaze
her bathing, this silvery retort

mercurially thus: *because I lay still
and did not cry they took me in hand*

all present admitting the presence of sweet air
as the scarecrow's faded clothes

mushy apples thrown to keep the dogs away
or tea

to rinse or clap your hands in flame
or beat your chest for hymns

the Huguenots' *flee, maintain, or die*
the screws of rhetoric that turn to iron

stalks of daikon I lay out for rollers
to make portable my savory beliefs

they are the legs soon popped and locked
as it is not enough to commit inside

instead the bag of the mouth
must fill with it with the good letter

so down goes dagon on top of me
my apostate beloved

I playne Piers which can not flatter
and kiss the canting doctor recanting

decanting or rather double canting
in the affirmative: it happened it happens to us

*

I am
found
that I am

*

in this garden I cannot see this shade
where the bride and groom keep pressing faces
trying to turn into sentiments as
wouldn't mind dying but I got to go by myself
and into something with significance
even hand grenades of an angry god
anything to make the love affair stop
possessed of those effects for which I
for no one may serve more than one master
and all the collection agents like trees
in the wandering forests look alike
just shy of familiar and treacherous
so that I am lost lord in the open
may one be pardoned and retain th' offence?

I'm conjured pure conspired against my rest
and couldn't die here now in the water
with no way to mark my election not
to mark my rest and not to own my rest
the burly balladeer
                    where he leads me

that I   from the top of the statue
should front   ressentiment   as those who laugh
in this life must cry in the next and so
I'm bound blind in this bind

there is no shade that I can see just ire
amazing, astounding, astonishing
as if the stone that's on my tongue inside
the sacrificial syllabus   for love

were incandescent too good to look at
because terrible or what kind of love
obliging songs destroys the strings and vents
to summon them and clean cauterize them
bathing or washing for what profits it
in this outfit to cast off the whole world
if profit is our motive who can stand
against us with dice in our mouths and psalms
the false morning off our pale naked skins
with blush running there to defend the front
calling reinforcements from the middle
or barracks in our trunks to hold our ground
no grave gonna hold my body down
perform the gripe of love when I am lost
astonished prone and out of my cold clothes
courted by angels courted by devils

*

the hart-of-grease retains the offence, stares into the face of the ham-faced man,
and bites the inside of his cheek   for the abolition of the offence I must behave
myself have myself behaved I mean like the ice cube tray and its metal lever in
the southern summer

and from there I crossed the woven waves, winter-sad, downcast for want of a
hall   lacking how's manifests the ship's wager that hull of cargo would make it
west my bond dissolved and the bath water slimy with cold cream and face paint

two handfuls of salt seeding the walking paths to prevent a costly slip (thinking
didn't they destroy all signs of life and salt the earth but weren't they the salt
of the earth the remnant as such that might have lost its flavor)   dealing means
giving and taking away   O give me a glimpse of our embrace if

exile's path awaits   not twisted gold

the masterless see the yellow waves before them, the sea-birds bathe, spread their
feathers, frost and snow fall mingled with hail that tender hymn's author John
Newton retained the offence, slave trader, and thought he'd felt the hand of god,
and no longer plied the trade, and still possessed the effects

Never   too hot-hearted, nor too hasty of speech, nor too fearful, nor too glad,
nor too greedy is the position of exile in the conditions of plenty because too is
the buzz in this giant yard too too   comin' 'round the mountain

    wait (too much to ask of me as I stare into the woven waves the yellow waves)
how can you wait for grace how could you know that it was coming

        when all the wealth of this world stands waste
and the buzz goes quiet

wait then   time to sleep when I'm dead   time to stop swimming when my mind
goes calm

and the price of a sandwich isn't *a wolf shared one with Death;   a man sad of
face hid in an earth-pit*

Here in the lawn of too here friend is fleeting, here man is fleeting, here woman
is fleeting—all this earthly habitation shall be emptied

                                        Where for us all stability resides   there
is the comfortably fitting protective plastic   the perfect retainer

the nation with no territory of kindness and waiting and less than too
to the kindness of no territory and its own special language
with words and also non-words   so two or more creatures might
stand together in companionable silence

that would be sweet

"Song #3"

crows everywhere
cruising
what turns up
in the thaw

I thought I was sure
until now
and no
in the wind

the art
of good dying:
all of the hands
in the bedclothes

and a strolling senses
and the letting downs

even
the stickerbush
has teeth
on its thorns

the cranberries
weighed down
like
the gilded
pills
of the pawnbrokers

with teeth

forgive me
the roots

or if that
is impossible

clear a place
by the sidewalk

a clearing
within the clearing

of the little lawn

set out my good shirt

This shirt is true bark. It sits cold and comfortable on the skin. In the rain it dries quickly. In the heat it breathes. In cold clothes. In this only house. Peeking at the gaps. The road rises to the stand of trees. It dips behind the house. The neighbors loom on the lawn in their shirts. They are looking past me and the house to the stars as if the house and I were protecting the stars. I am in their way. My shirt is.

Under the lid of the house: resonating. Hammer strike at doors and windows is a conversion. In this violence, player and instrument keep tuning into each other. *Aye, and that's because there's a sounding board; and what in all things makes the sounding-board in this—there's naught beneath. And yet a coffin with a body in it rings pretty much the same, Carpenter.*

The giant oak transistor. Assorted chairs. The ironing board woven between planks. This incidental music is all and blue.

"Special Rider Blues"

It is the special circumstance of abundance
and abjection that makes for the blues

only modifying things
nothing under our boot-soles
only the troubled muddled
and hectoring of modify
your NO your YES
when hailing pleasure is hailing pain

a cautious lot, cocking the head in such a way
you didn't know if you were being greeted
or being shunned
struck twice by lightning
twice in the american place

modification and sameness : kith and cruel wool
united states of metamorphosis

*

In the giant lawn lightning struck
Or the giant pond lightning threaded
modifying

you have to have a lot of patience
with bureaucracy to live in a river

speak hear see here touch this pulsive community
chartered by fathers fingering the humane
the men who had preceded them had rendered in-between things
more clearly, bringing into focus the gradients that connected
this to that, showing how you got from here to there
this patrimony tho
with *everything in between missing or, at best, out of focus*
that this ground be under something legal
fungible
with many cells

*

what these blues is
between two seams
sames a long styrofoam plateau
on this parenthesis
"take this message to the other side"

on
this long lonesome loft
from that
between NO and YES
of forever roll-over revolver

the garden is open to visitors between

The body knows where it is in space. It tells the mind more or less. The body is very far from the stars the body says to the mind. Sometimes things recede. Timing goes awry. Because doing something is always a resurrection, things tend to be done poorly. Driving a car feels like driving a person who is driving a car.

I'm trying to raise my hand in greeting, but my hand is choking you. Sorry. I'm on the long road of a lawn. "It is human nature to stand in the middle of a thing, / but you cannot stand in the middle of this," says the mind or the body. In the tide of the road, where things get done: lying down and getting up.

The drive washes through the cemetery. The ground is all uneven, gullied at a tight bend that trails down and away, back to the main road. Like any place, the cemetery has ways leading in and ways leading out. The driveway is sometimes a waterway. Entrance. Exit. Head. Mouth.

"Dvorak"

What   I   do

I do   it   quickly
although

in a bedtime

in the wrinkled paper
we've been pulling over us

about a mile from town
I picked a stick up

flatted third
flatted fifth

then what   what will that sound like

small,
        frail,
                bespectacled

afloat on the weave democracy
with heavy eyes already
trickster tale   murder ballad   when we begin to mourn

drawn in the pine dust
by the shoulders
and key generations

a country girl in white clothes
fleck and also clump
of pine

*

as one studies apocalypse and history
        one begins to suspect the latter was never
        anything but a distended category
        of the former

the long ditch tennessee sewer we   small
smoking drinking with tongues   frail
falling out in the pentecost
off the map by warp of fraying screen
little sister   bespectacled
of the razorback
of tom dooley hanging his head
ants churning at the base of the tree

when we have   made our parade
and squiggles
   and mush

the law here
letter leaded (poor religious animal)

so besooted so covered in soot
they had to pull her stocking down

in the pencil factory
in marietta   of a carpet bag

*

          I met her on a mountain, there I took her life or
    knoxville girl
little sister

I took her   golden curls
thrown her into the river
that flows through knoxville town

    small

what is what stands where

    frail

I beat her down   I caught her

*

noise from the news's world
the form of the new like antlers and skin

I kept in a carpetbag
with sprinklers and the cotton plague

I met my little sadie and I shot her down

on the mountain by the river
hydraulic as they call their quicksand

with a band around one   in the corner
that his blood might wash over   constitutionally
or in other words   our mouths don't make   for cutting
what we mash anyway

in this special circumstance
of novelty where I put my full hand   in the perfect
blues of
some warm rigor or more rigorous persuasions

retaining wall

blind oconaluftee rhododendron bloom
the blues all in your bread

what we take   as a kindness
gone sour down the bluff
bagged
    tagged

summoning years of physical and spiritual training
like brass tears clink clink

*

in the sedge grass
the little white rig
that I walked to
where I saw the hawk
and the raft in the sun:
forbidding angel

I brought my lover to the tree
I brought my angel him me
hang your head tom dooley

*

this stuff colloquial   with tongues in dust
by stuff of high prophecy   but where can
with what hole *his stretched sinews taught*
taut? To breaking all strings
his blue gray playing
what key   to be american in the morning
and an american conversation is the colloquy asleep
to live with the act of living with *conversatio*
to turn about with in bed with the american
conversation of mutation   heraklitus spins so fast
I use him for a drill
the blues

the mutilation blues
have before behave

"Jesus is a Dying Bedmaker #2"

gallery galley galleon gallows
the shallows   the gentlemen of the pit
even to the uttermost part & co.

an acre or a refuge for her Inhabitants, so as man, who is the earth we
treade upon, & of habitation, etc, (many men spending

your
little Sister,
this Plantation

                & we stand striving here more willingly in another Country)
& thus it will be a worke of Land, it would procure them of theire

                                                        trail

your little sister this long yard you run

                coming upon us, whom he hath provided this Plantation, for
places of man to lie waste without any such as are forced by

mission tidewater   the sheet my lord pulls
beneath my chin as I am shivering

*

lord should faith give me something given
to stand on plant on grow on   own defend
turn my skin into   turn into my skin

this american gift   the tidewater
should I be hidden in the tidewater

what confluence of singing and mourning
what gospel blues   meaning good news gone bad
without the benefit of fantasies
of heaven   or even the high prospect
of being
right

once the colony has foundered

being between quarks   being between zeitgeists
being between malaises   being angstrom'd out

vertebra by vertebra by this old
hollers of us   there goes the neighborhood
down to lesbos   singing all this death blues

because I am cold in these clothes despicable day respectable day
sun cloud sun rain lonesome at home star cloud leaf cloud
staring across the lanes into that lonesome yard getting mowed
overgrowing covered in snow sunburned cloudy under
shadows of wires   splat with crabgrass here and there
getting plowed in the sun where once was sea that guy
my neighbor who wears handkerchiefs always cutting hedges
always by always as "some infinite thing" like the waters

and the patriotic hunker—as in I will always be I
in this head or out of it jesus my head full of waters
my american head I must not park on dry grass or leaves
have I always believed or was I converted—towards
what conversations await   what customs

some children are left

            to the history of belief which is
me asking is my faith like this set of claws phonograph
skipping in the run out groove of sgt. peppers never
could see any other way

for every man that prints adventures
apropos of the uttermost parts of the earth which is
a stage where are performed acts   and gentile darknesses

in places speeches made in the east telegraphed west
to the Naturals of the place   not arriving but partially
arrived   not ascending but one foot in the clouds

cum actu ascendisset so *men tye lead to their feet*
and when they are laying hand-fast upon Abrahams
bosome, they must pull their hand to obey importunities

IN this world OR OF this world   in other words…
if you seeke to establish a temporall kingdome
you are not rectified liberty needing no one, &c.

O, if you could once bring a catechisme to bee as
good ware amongst them as a bugle, as a knife, as a hatchet

if you could submit yourself tidewater missionary
to mother lover jesus turning down the bed
a friendly voice said
you could submit to anything and have more joy

awash in my banalities
giggling from the teeth outward
I am of this world but seldom
in it

not the big lawn nothing but real estate
lots of citizens little tidewater

*

because *GOD bindes not himself to measures*
GOD bindes not himself to times

and now is the time is upon us
as the plantation has flourished
its inhabitants converted
or modified
or comforted to sleep

and its inhabitance an easy thing
liver and spleen
in the wilderness in the wilderness

one, &c. O, if profit is the needles eye
the mouth must not, how mourn then more american bone

The table and *coup de marriage* set out. The incorruptible bread with a fly on it. It's the water in the veins makes our manners and the blood all over the place. A courtesy all over the neighbors. Sticking to the lawn. In weird places: hands and arms up to the elbows and also in a sticky bib around the neck. Is it so simple, living is eating? A kind of life. The loved ones take with the strangers. The neighborly way as in nature: the peace in the eyes, savoring the pieces.

"Finale"

The cleanest poisons
            ever are ours
even-toned   in layers
trust   worthy
    bound by
the stainless view

the taste of heterocycles

the luculent burnt crust
    that edges nothing
has no edge

no guru no
method no
teacher no

almondbreadcaramelcinnamonfattyhoneymeatoilypungentrancidsweet
made from corncobs

and other waste products

a solvent and fungicide

upon exposure to air it turns dark brown or black

furfural
    folderol

also used in
    the fabrication of
        fiberglass and
automobile brake pads

It foretells the wheat
that is not wheat
but our convertible
in our nostrils
toward
the end
furfural
            folderol
thiazole

the smell of burning
houses on the air
the taste of them
on the tongue
as
    a
message mixes
so
    a medium-
sized circuit
may mislead

clear to pale yellow

harmful if swallowed
        flammable
     folderol
thiazole

bread alone or nutty meaty mocha

but great for
                dyeing
                        cotton

can you hear
your bread

on fire for wild ranges
     green senses burnt senses

or
unity
in finale

fall's folderol's
     chemical song
we're all done
but not all full

eat this odor tidewater
winding sheet

furfural
        thiazole

folderol
      we need another idle tune for
      pyrrolines
      thiophenes
      pyrazines
flummery   fiddle
         dee
           deem

to famines
   love's famines
      off the icebox
herald horn of flats
to green-sweet
   a honey-like

common to petroleum
   irritates eyes and skin

do you smell sulfur
           darling?

so seem is the finale
the taste
    the smell
        the seams to seem

and what do you see
        fiddle
         deem

pyrroline

thiophene   thiophene

pyrazine   pyrazine

pyrroline

and what do you taste
        and what do you smell
when the day
        is
    accomplished

"America"

faces: for deficient [--] Physique should

THE MISTRESS, and alchemy this

returns of charity and fierce with

and derived for knowledge and

of life. The sciences flourish,

this beyond others; and malignant

deficient, though of letters is

conforming to the rule that beauty

is a strange attractor. Should

the Physique be wanting, something else

will step in [--] mind

THE beauty of mind contained

in MISTRESSed matter even garbage

on the road to Ohio

and alchemy this returns of

others and malignant deficient, though of

your learned governors. For like waters

faith, as moralities, as human judgment

human learning stood upon

alchemy this returns of life

a strange attractor Should the Physique be

there is a remainder

unrighteous rim of what stood

details upon details ash upon asphodel

what destroys learning making it

see the alchemy of sight cooking off

the hotdogs the bbq grill

mercury rising like a hell river

will step in learned governors. For

learning making it see the road

light or contemplation thoroughly, but

gather by importunity, and thereupon said:

of invention, for surely rich

though of others and malignant deficient,

waters faith, as human learning

letters in stone or metal

provide a way to begin simply

of particulars within a limit

and arbitrary as the bat boy bunts

beyond the cave's rim

thereupon others said: believe

yourself enough to doubt yourself

is letters is letters is details

upon details upon asphodel what

knowledge, which give himself but

to balance with it was

same abuses; at first,

Should the alchemy of in [--]

this return of particulars within a

life devoted to its dwelling

in a metal trap on springs

hands on wheel lights on road

we're sitting in the operahouse

expectancy or ecstasy expectancy ecstasy

outside the provision let's go

the village cornet band provides

in learned governors. For like waters

the bbq grill mercury rising

from master Socrates, whom they

So unto Domitian in games

a dimension and all other terrene and

yourself enough to balance with

knowledge and malignant deficient, though

not murderous shy of fierce

-ness in the lawn not bloody

with gore blood and cold or warm

with accounts or checks and Balances of

the human body   micropolis my temple

splitting at the temple delivering the goods

and reconciling the bill with someone

not His approach and   is a dying evening light

like waters faith, as the bat   after walking here making calls here

not bloody with someone   learning what troubles the clean air

metal provide a remainder unrighteous   washed of that history in stacks

and Balances of letters is   records gone all that listing

springs hands on wheel lights   of love with hate we've felt

is greater than duty which   destroys with for mingling of curves with knowledge and alchemy of sight

springs hands on road light or

of how rarely all

be delivered; for understanding

think considering it requires more
unlawful

laws to begin simply will

life a dimension and cold or

beyond feeling the "flow state" opens

the skin of the subject and

take a long hard look this passes

with sentences with séances with

silences blazons chattering weeping

a study in scissors truss

my blue faith is another's alchemy

a metal provides a hell river

to the subject and balances of what

or cherishing of prenotion

EADEM FECERIS CIRUS SOMNUS LUDUS PER

pertaineth to affirm that moral virtues

a dimension and alchemy of others

of that history in the human body

It always plays eats and sleeps

the same as making calls here

after the trip to hell

on the subject of hell travel

keep moving   you'll get back eventually

to the here of here

the same life (sleeping eating playing) calls

No grave can hold my body down
no body can hold my grave body
my embarrassed body must die
down body cannot hold down
even gravity only loves it
       can only touch it lovingly
as the body kisses the top of the road
odd owning my down body
that cannot be owned that is held down
like holding down a job is owning
eventually it rises to the occasion
the disembodied occasion the grave
lies down for that is walking upright
walking out on the job of the body
stealing away with the body on
as even the responsibilities of the grave
can hold without holding down

"Dalhart, Texas, 1967"

The ground is humiliating
sometimes I'm bound to crawl on it

to crawl into the low windows
the rest being
          gone

          the ground sand restlessness
after every sand rope halfunbinding

so good morning of affliction
after particulars of shame

          a news

in my carpetbag   I mean in

my heart

*

which is why the travel story
is the one   exile of patriot
    one bad shell
roaming lump humiliation
leads

        to new methodism

drinking your own pee, for example

as opposed to walking
                        into the ground

for it

and a song: this color of a fever, this color of a cold
            this hole leads to the river
            we're calling this hole home

seen from the up here, Dalhart is where
the southern crosses the northern
amid grass rings like bubbles

rising to more texas

    Jess Morris *leaving cheyenne*
                goodbye old paint
goodbye circular field irrigation

    *

on the ground is
in the ground is

for setting a course by augers is
upsetting a course by augers as

and I would travel in
my country   *old*

              paint

     to a safe way   as safe as we can hope for
based on where we've been

how far   off course   our abrahamming
'discoursing as the world would of such
an action   divers ways'
off of 'intimate impulses'

riding the line through lonely stretches
like others, its rhythm comes from the movement of a horse

many of these songs may show some hard edges, and,
              they may fail to please,
but I am confident that the class I address
will not find them exaggerated,
nothing extenuated, nor aught
set down in malice
which is why the travel story is the one
and also not the one

*

erroneous republic
        wondering the way ·
                through the tune

this morning blues all around
    my bed

        I want to cross the river of jordan in my heart

        the timing kind of cracked
neither to the horse nor the metronome

to the weaving water & dust

Which is the test not the testimony of your
                        yes/no

                for the good of the whole bodie;
                as the office of the eie is to see,
                the eare to heare, and the foot to goe

walk while its light:
work while it is day

walk worthy

between the vespers of history

        *

We bring the rolling ink position not
the interstate speed but the hunt and peck
and peck and gathering wander economy

paint   scratch   chickens and dogs
            goats and

I gather you mean I assume you mean
I weave the nation into the sense of
closure not rich enough   never rich

of thoreau's false etymologies:
sans terre . . . the secret of successful sauntering
without cracks not lachrymose

clear-eyed and whole   gathering speed
in love with the paradox of moving
of the city *à pied* to find
good songs variations
so as to perform
the duty

*and what I have been preparing to say
is, that in Wildness is the preservation
of the World.*

*

I shall now tell you about the quickest way to Jerusalem. For some folk do not want to use the other route – some because they have not enough money, some because they have not enough people to go with, some because they cannot stand a long journey, some because they fear the dangers of the deserts, some . . . But I will go back and tell you of other routes that can be followed, keeping more to dry land – useful for those who cannot endure traveling by sea, but prefer to go by land even if it is more trouble. [You make your way] to one of the ports of
A man crosses the sea to
From there he goes to   and crosses the stretch of water called   Thence he goes by land to
then he goes to
He will pass through

Thence men go through the hills of   the vales of   the open moors; one passes the town of   or the towns that stand on the great and noble rivers   There are many fine hills in those parts, many fair woods and great plenty of wild game to hunt.

He who wants to go a different way will go through the plains of   On that coast is   Further up in the mountains is a fine city called   When a man has crossed these mountains and moors, he goes through the city of   where there is a great bridge over   a great river, which is navigable; it runs fast from the mountains to   Near the city of   is another river that comes from the   At the crossing of this river Saint   lost his wife and two children. This river runs through the plain of   Thence men go to the city of   where there are hot springs and hot baths. There are many fine woods. From you go to a city called

then to

and then to

and from there are two ways to Jerusalem, one to the left and the other to the right.

The dead are serious about the metaphors of living. Death is synec-
dochic. They lust murderously for a lover. A piece of a lover. *O that
I had my Beloved I would not let him go, but he should lye all night
betwixt my breasts!* I have woken in cold sheets alone in dark winter
morning knowing *I held Him and would not let Him go,* knowing he
lay *all night as a bundle of myrrh between my breasts,* a dead lover.
I've followed the walking dead.

"Knoxville Blues"

Which was the fantasia

        as the preservation of the world is wildness
                and what is wild
                has no use for sympathetic stories

and all we want and don't want of us
is in the singing

        wandering to
                preserve
the singing that has no use

for wildness wilderness and innocence
are inconsistent notions   there's only trauma and
                                        help or harm
                                                in it
                                                        the black sap rotten knot

to clean song (two house sparrows sing at one another)

        and what lies behind their singing is
        a metaphor for wildness in domesticity (*passer domesticus,*
        or HOSP, sometimes called the English Sparrow)

we've been through this garden
superfluous branches / we lop away, that bearing bows may live

Which was the fantasia

*

mourning and pleading most mild

                     so mild as a fever always

an even ferocity   the grass coming in

the fever of tuning

this even ferocity of nature

*

what kind of creation

the kind that interrupts

        river interrupted
        river flood
        measures the river
        love not love
        the river mark
        line of mold
        mould of make
        edge and fold
        river interrupted
        river flood
        measures the river
        love not love

not help not harm not not not
I said I would not say no
help me with my disbelief

    a hero perish a sparrow fall

*

thought every degree of creation
            a degree of evil thought and every
            thought degree of evil a degree of unbeing

        coming through these degrees
        flying the finale we at a crux in the world

even as I was yanking the sparrow's nest
from the gutter pipe a metaphor for help and harm
was up there and the thunder rushing me

                pass domicile
                pestering as you must be
                terminal tearing

"Mark 1:15"

eschatology in
          every choice now
that the kingdom

     at empire's end

          that the end of choices
is to hand as one chooses with the hand
and something is

fulfilled for help or harm

repent ye   from *poena* pain trauma or

turn you little apocalyptic band
orbiting a sun
          on a lined planet
from left to breathing   *trikonasana*

lord, I cannot believe in   damnation
only salvation from trouble in mind
               but
                  there
               is fruit,
             And thou
hast hands

and all I know of heaven is this
backward view of paradise   all I know of hell
          so I am damned and living

loving my damnation but letting go a little

from call to call

or to turn   this verse   the time is full
with happenings straight over the lip of it
until the coyote looks down

and there's another lesson from history
it also rises and falls

*

that *culpa*   I cop to   yes lord
I see the ground

    coming for to poof of dust

and sorry I am lord sorry I am
so as I spin from turning   conscience bit

but the gospel in the gospel is the thing is done
except for doings

prayer not swimming in the lippes
                          but groaned out
         (and *thy will? maketh intercession*
                for us with groanings that cannot
                be uttered)
not greatly in sight
abhorred everywhere
             yet notwithstanding
the same silly flocke so despised

no judgment save in always   how the wave chooses beginnings
                and endings   the pluck of a string

such that good evil being born dying tempo
dynamo dolorolorolo
an elegant vacuum fluctuation model

97

the saddle of the guitar
the saddle of the people of the saddle
these end-of-the-world blues

in a pink housecoat, staggering along the sidewalk
is how the time's fulfilled and the kingdom of God at hand

       the sparrow can crush you

chatter chatter twitch
empty headed angel of destruction
landed in my gutter rail

to say there is no time
and if there is a God, God's *rationale* is nobody's business
but

Savasana the corpse at the end of the runway

*

I thought I heard one whisper:
              from this garden see the other gardens
              the two valleys terraced with them
              sinking in the shadows of late afternoon
              and what do you see
                            but what is a garden

              whether the moon and humid night
              turning to early blue or the empty sky
              everything at hand the short yard dotted
              in strawberry clover
                      this and the pools in the storm

              write out this…

the ground you stand on being formed
by waves   the slowest ululations of stone
so the garden is a furrow   as the furrow
is a garden   and all reflecting God's
stern brow at hand   five fingers six strings
wheat which looks like tares   tares which look
like wheat
let them go anywhere they may / till that great harvest day

the great agriculturalist bias of these metaphors
we are not seeds   or produce
would you wrinkle us like soda cans?

*

in the worn way between the sidewalks
telling the puddles to dry up
and the dry spots to become puddles
or the patches of shade to curl
Jesus help me die before I die

bore me Jesus to death
to adoration of what is boring
being disconnected and so more real
            the driveshaft of the delivery truck
            beside me clanking coming apart
            from my day
            pulling my day apart with a lurch
            and crotchety spin

*

in the behaviors
clapboard and latticed havens abuzz with soot flies
     sundry voices wheeling
out of weeding   walking rows shaking
seed   watering (stream shower mist)
so that seeing this I'm seeing nothing
and my head is filled with chatter:
               this friend leaving this friend
grass seed cloud   the crabgrass say I hate you
and I say I hate you crabgrass
     S of water   this levee breached this levee holding
sulfur and entropy   john faustus
holy desire   sacred despair   canary mums
     another friend taking an apartment and another
grasping the receiver

of this heaven   third suspended heaven
about us

*

a cage of carbon
a cage of saxophones
a cage of tagged fish
a cage of stone piers
a cage of wide red ribbons
a cage of live and dead cats at the Moran market where cats are
sold to make soup
a cage of split palm stem
a cage of every unclean and hateful bird

say the passing beauties to the root of my tongue to
                    the learned doctors I'm robed in

the tribulations of being narrated
          by soft radio voices or calling the cosy house
you left your lover with   these minutes seconds of
                    unveiling
      the voice of the sparrow
              of the turtledove

To what place? Is that my breath on the glass?

In the light of day, the birds in the street, the air. The birds on the branches.
Is it flies?

Is it a burning service station? A spot of color on the night?

After a storm, it's all littered with branches. We gather them for kindling.
After the winter, every color of tulip, encaustic by the roadside.

The father. The husband.

The son. The true vine.

But the American parable is not quite like this.

We are the people,

> those people shuffling across the lawn.

"Voice of the Turtle"

John the Baptist said
you must be all voice

in habit, diet, dwelling, conversation, preaching

a voice in the furrow and a voice in the yoke

my love your beast of burden
my lord my love

I confess.
Sometimes I look at the face of my beloved and say
to myself *see her   see the object of your love in time*
and can only half succeed or worse

being so bad at time
          and proverbs

as the empty garden wilts
                    giant blossoms curling on the ground
and colossal gourds in knots softening

for to hear is to know that something grows
still the worm and spontaneous along
the hard plastic case protecting the fruit
and seeds from the worm or the drawling word
drawing close while you nap in the garden
in the mild shade of the rusty plane tree
covered in catkin buttons or humid

the porches of your ears in open air

into the adversary's singing
in the hide of the hound

the *vafer*, barker, coney catcher, bull-baiter:
                come come

riders winding their horns as they go

singing words around the brick foot of town
to my strangling to get out of its sight
and into a safer part of the lawn

where its eyes don't read and its matted coat
doesn't isn't not so fell with briars

back to: *nostos algos* homecoming grief
to the ground where my work is sore not sad

even with the turnspit grinning at us
licking its chops while we trim azalea
(take care)

learn to die
learning G: *as runs the Glass, | man's life doth pass*
                X: *Xerxes did die, | and so must you and I*
                Y: *Youth forward slips, | death soonest nips*

the intimacy of the stale bedclothes
the intimacy of the stale hair
the intimacy of the stale t-shirt   the senescent details
in which the devil is not

but looks on from a bank not far off

down on the garden streets
the right angle of the pigeon wing
stretching out from the parking lot
means something got to the pigeon
but this is not evil evil is how we love
this burdened pear tree we love

since we do not await the resurrection of the dead
since we are the already resurrected dead
        that resurrection we are awaiting
        has come but we do not recognize it

and instead burrow into the sinus
of what we think we saw on our way over
of what we were positive we saw
though we could hardly bear to look
because we say we shouldn't

the vast sinus of memory we tend at work
the curve, fold, hollow, coil   genital hiding place
Lord of this church of America that is and is not
the love song I sing and the hymn

or is it the other way
        obsessed not possessed   Yeats:
        The three-fold terror of love; a fallen flare
        Through the hollow of an ear

that devil paul who I am
I am singing back through the horn of
through the testaments
to my own undertone

convertible   capable of love so
so facing death-in-life

Oh violent lover Christ with the kisses of your mouth
make haste keeper of not kept vineyards
our not kept couch
the not kept beams of our house
our not kept rafters

the vines on vines on vines
brutal boy I find you not for vines
washed in the blood
in the blossoms of the vines

> *your eyes*
> *your hair*
> *your teeth*
> *like the blood*
> *thread*
> *your cheek*
> *your neck*
> *your breast*
> *your den of lions*
> *your mountain of tigers*

my failing soul you mean
terrible as an army with banners
coming up from the wilderness
as death is strong as love
the grave as fierce as passion

"The Waltz That Carried Us Away
and Then a Mosquito Came Up
and Ate My Sweetheart"

Ever since we've been managed
in the footfalls: our time of dying
day is done / gone the sun lullaby

For example, when Christ arises from the dead,
He is free from the grave;
and yet the grave remains.

Peter is liberated from prison,
　　　and the paralytic from his bed,
　　　　　the young man from his coffin,
　　　　　　　the girl from her couch;
　　nevertheless, the prison,
　　　　　　　the bed,
　　　　　　　　　the coffin,
　　　　　and the couch remain.

So also the Law is abrogated when I am freed from it,
and the Law dies when I have died to it;

and yet the Law still remains

Aaron McCollough was raised in Tennessee. He is the Librarian for English Literature and Comparative Literature at the University of Michigan. His previous books for Ahsahta Press are *Little Ease* (2006) and *Welkin* (2002), which was the first winner of the Saw- tooth Poetry Prize.

AHSAHTA PRESS

SAWTOOTH POETRY PRIZE SERIES

2002: Aaron McCollough, *Welkin* (Brenda Hillman, judge)

2003: Graham Foust, *Leave the Room to Itself* (Joe Wenderoth, judge)

2004: Noah Eli Gordon, *The Area of Sound Called the Subtone* (Claudia Rankine, judge)

2005: Karla Kelsey, *Knowledge, Forms, The Aviary* (Carolyn Forché, judge)

2006: Paige Ackerson-Kiely, *In No One's Land* (D. A. Powell, judge)

2007: Rusty Morrison, *the true keeps calm biding its story* (Peter Gizzi, judge)

2008: Barbara Maloutas, *the whole Marie* (C. D. Wright, judge)

2009: Julie Carr, *100 Notes on Violence* (Rae Armantrout, judge)

2010: James Meetze, *Dayglo* (Terrance Hayes, judge)

Aaron McCollough was raised in Tennessee. He is the Librarian for English Literature and Comparative Literature at the University of Michigan. His previous books for Ahsahta Press are *Little Ease* (2006) and *Welkin* (2002), which was the first winner of the Sawtooth Poetry Prize.

AHSAHTA PRESS

SAWTOOTH POETRY PRIZE SERIES

2002: Aaron McCollough, *Welkin* (Brenda Hillman, judge)

2003: Graham Foust, *Leave the Room to Itself* (Joe Wenderoth, judge)

2004: Noah Eli Gordon, *The Area of Sound Called the Subtone* (Claudia Rankine, judge)

2005: Karla Kelsey, *Knowledge, Forms, The Aviary* (Carolyn Forché, judge)

2006: Paige Ackerson-Kiely, *In No One's Land* (D. A. Powell, judge)

2007: Rusty Morrison, *the true keeps calm biding its story* (Peter Gizzi, judge)

2008: Barbara Maloutas, *the whole Marie* (C. D. Wright, judge)

2009: Julie Carr, *100 Notes on Violence* (Rae Armantrout, judge)

2010: James Meetze, *Dayglo* (Terrance Hayes, judge)

This book is set in Apollo MT type
with Titling Gothic FB Skyline and Apollo titles
by Ahsahta Press at Boise State University
Cover design by Quemadura.
Cover photograph © Black River Productions, Ltd. / Mitch Epstein.
Courtesy of Sikkema Jenkins & Co., New York.
Used with permission. All rights reserved.
Book design by Janet Holmes.

AHSAHTA PRESS

2011

JANET HOLMES, DIRECTOR
JODI CHILSON, MANAGING EDITOR

KYLE CRAWFORD

CHARLES GABEL

KATE HOLLAND

WALLY HUMPHRIES

TORIN JENSEN

JESSICA JOHNSON, *intern*

GENNA KOHLHARDT

JULIE STRAND

JASON STEPHENS, *intern*

MATT TRUSLOW

ZACH VESPER